Fight Your Virginia Reckless Driving Ticket

ANDREW FLUSCHE

Andrew Flusche, Attorney at Law, PLC
www.AndrewFlusche.com
540.318.5824

Thank you for taking the time to read my book! I'm Andrew Flusche, and I've helped hundreds of drivers fight their Virginia reckless driving charges. I always strive for the best possible result in court with the least amount of stress for my clients.

Andrew

Dedication

To my amazing wife,
for her unending love and support.

Disclaimer

I'm a lawyer.
You knew there'd be a disclaimer, didn't you?

This book is educational information only.
This is not legal advice.

ANY CASE RESULTS INCLUDED IN THIS BOOK
ARE BASED ON THE SPECIFIC FACTS OF
THOSE CASES. PAST RESULTS DO NOT
PREDICT FUTURE SUCCESS.

Praise from Past Clients

"Andrew is a wonderful lawyer. I never had a need for a lawyer before, so I was unsure about who to trust with my case and the overall process it entailed. I am so grateful to have had Andrew as my lawyer. I appreciated his prompt and genuine communication and guidance with me throughout the entire process. He was professional and kind, and I can honestly say I will pass along his name to those I know."
-- Laura

"Great communication and follow through! Knowledgeable and knows how to get the job done. Took care of everything for me regarding my ticket, I had to do NOTHING. Thank you!"
-- Lindsay

"Sometimes people want just a little hand with there situation. Welcome to the big hand. When talking with Andrew I could feel the assurance that he was going to do best possible job for me and my problem. He was going to bring good results with a smile. Your name will definitely be passed around. Thanks again."
-- Robert

"Facing a serious traffic violation can seem very daunting. Andrew helped lessen my anxiety by providing excellent representation. He is friendly, responsive, professional, and most importantly, he achieved the best possible result for my case. I would gladly recommend him to anyone seeking counsel."
-- Anne

Contents

Introduction

If you're reading this book, you are probably charged with Virginia reckless driving. You may have a barrage of advertising being thrown at you. It's confusing and possibly scary.

You are not alone.

You're holding the key to understanding your charge, possible defenses, what might happen in court, and how to select an attorney for your case. It's all right here.

I suggest sitting down in your favorite chair with a cup of coffee or tea and diving right in. When you're done reading, you'll have a clearer picture of how to handle your case.

1. What is reckless driving?

Reckless driving is a class 1 **misdemeanor** in Virginia. It's the same level of offense as DUI. You read that right. A person who gets involved in an accident or speeds a little too fast is charged with a misdemeanor on the same plane as DUI.

Virginia has many different types of reckless driving. To understand your case, you first have to start with the ticket itself. It's the piece of paper you received from the officer that usually says "Virginia Uniform Summons" at the top. In most cases, they're yellow carbon copies.

The summons will show the section of the Virginia Code (or local ordinance) that you're charged with violating. There are 14 different types of reckless driving, but they do not all come up often in court. Here are the most common varieties:

Reckless by speed – Most reckless driving tickets are based solely on speed. In Virginia, any speed over 80 miles per hour, or any speed 20 miles per hour or more above the speed limit, qualifies as reckless driving (VA Code § 46.2-862). Since some interstates in Virginia have 70-mile-per-hour speed limits, you could be charged with reckless driving for going only 11 miles-per-hour over the limit.

Failure to maintain control – When an accident occurs, the State Police typically charge the person they think caused the accident with failure to maintain control (VA Code § 46.2-853). This shows why you should read your ticket carefully. Many people get a ticket that just says "failure to maintain control," only to be surprised when they later find out it's for reckless driving.

Passing a stopped school bus – If an officer thinks you passed a school bus while it was stopped for loading / unloading children, you could get a reckless driving ticket (VA Code § 46.2-859). The code section for this version requires the Commonwealth to prove a number of specific items, including the color of the bus. Judges certainly take these sorts of tickets seriously, due to the possible danger to children.

General – Even if your driving behavior did not fit one of the many specific definitions of reckless driving, you could be charged under the catch-all statute if your driving allegedly endangered people or property (VA Code § 46.2-852). This section can be charged in a wide variety of situations from doing wheelies on a motorcycle to passing in a "no passing" zone.

Importantly, you shouldn't get too focused on the term "reckless driving." In Virginia, you don't have to be truly driving in a reckless manner to be charged with "reckless driving." As we just saw, you can be charged with this offense simply due to exceeding the speed limit by a designated amount, even if you were otherwise driving 100% safely.

Regardless which version your ticket says, it's still a criminal charge. That means you'll have a court date, be asked to enter a plea, and there will be a trial. The Commonwealth has to prove that you are guilty beyond a reasonable doubt. It's not like you've seen on *Law & Order*, but it's a real trial that affects your life!

Throughout the next few chapters, we'll go through an overview of a Virginia reckless driving case. We'll look at what you're *really* facing including the possible long-term consequences. Then we'll examine defenses – the good ones, and the ineffective ones. After that, we'll see how you might be able to get the charge reduced or dismissed, even if the Commonwealth can prove the case.

Chapters 6 and 7 will cover the practical aspects of appearing in court and noting an appeal if things don't go the way you want. And we'll finish up the discussion with critical information on how to select an attorney to defend your case.

2. What are the consequences?

Here's where the rubber meets the road. Reckless driving carries a variety of possible punishments and serious long-term consequences.

Punishments

If you're convicted as charged, you could receive any combination of:

- Fine up to $2,500
- License suspension up to 6 months
- Jail up to 12 months

Your specific punishment will vary based on the facts of your case, your driving record, and the local judge who hears your case. But let's look at each one of the possible punishments.

Jail

Yes, JAIL is a possible punishment for Virginia reckless driving.

But let me tell it to you straight: most people don't go to jail for their reckless ticket. You'll see websites that claim ALL cases over 90 mph carry a risk of jail. That's simply not true across the board.

The courts where I practice (primarily Fredericksburg, Stafford, and Spotsylvania) typically do not impose jail time until at least 95 mph and usually only at 100 mph (or 30+ over the speed limit). That varies depending upon the judge and many other factors, but 90 is *not* the normal jail threshold in my area.

Why then do attorneys claim that? I hope it's ignorance, but I'm concerned some people may be trying to use scare tactics. Reckless driving is certainly serious, but it's stressful enough without having attorneys scaring you into hiring them.

Some areas of Virginia do use 90 mph as a jail threshold, but it's important to understand that every case differs. You're not automatically going to jail even if a particular judge uses a certain speed as a line in the sand.

The differences in jail time make it critically important to discuss your case with an attorney who knows the local players involved in your case.

License suspension

Next to jail, most people that I talk to are concerned about losing their license. After all, it's hard to get around most of the United States without being able to drive.

Fortunately, license suspension is similar to jail time. It doesn't happen in the average reckless driving case, but it's always possible, especially in higher speed cases.

In cases where the judge suspends your driver's license, he can authorize a restricted license. This gives you permission to drive for specific purposes, such as going to work, attending school, taking your children to school, and going to the doctor. A restricted license doesn't give you blanket permission to drive whenever you want, but it can at least help you get to work.

Fine

How much are you looking at paying? Good question. This one gets a little tougher to answer. Like jail and license suspension, the specific fine will depend upon a variety of factors including the local court.

The maximum $2,500 fine isn't used often that I see. Depending upon all the facts of the case, an average reckless driving fine could be in the neighborhood of $300 to $1,000. Definitely pricey. And then of course you have to add on court costs, which are about $80.

Some judges have rules of thumb for the fine. For example, a local Fredericksburg-area judge typically imposes $10 for each mph over the speed limit. Using that guide, a reckless driving conviction for 90 in a 65 mph zone would be a $250 fine plus court costs of $81.

Virginia law gives you at least 30 days to pay anything you owe to the court. If you need additional time, you can ask the court for a longer payment deadline.

But these are just the court-imposed punishments. What other consequences might you be facing if you're convicted of reckless driving? Here are a few to consider:

Long-term consequences

Insurance premium hike

Aside from fines, jail, and license suspension, insurance premiums are a major concern for many drivers. What will a reckless driving conviction due to your insurance premiums?

I always recommend calling your insurance company to find out. But some people worry about tipping them off to the pending ticket, so that may be a concern for you.

If you want an estimate, some data exists. According to one insurance survey, **a reckless driving conviction increases premiums on average by 21.8%!** A regular speeding ticket for 1-14 mph over the limit only increases premiums 10.62% on average.

Using those numbers, if you're currently paying $100 per month for insurance, **a reckless driving conviction would cost you $261 more per year in insurance premiums alone.** If the insurance company considers the conviction for multiple years, the expense gets worse. Hiring an attorney certainly costs some money up front, but avoiding a reckless driving conviction could easily save money in the long run.

Security clearance problems

Practicing near D.C., I've represented many people who were concerned about their security clearance. Rightfully so.

Your supervisor or security clearance review officer will know the best answer for your situation and clearance level, but any misdemeanor conviction could threaten a clearance. Based on my experience, one reckless driving conviction usually does not kill a clearance. However, multiple convictions could be seen as a judgment problem. But you will certainly need to speak with your clearance review officer to know the best route for your job security.

Loss of job

If you have to drive for a living or are on company insurance for occasional errands, your supervisor probably will not want to find out about a reckless driving conviction. Some companies have rules that require terminating employees based on their driving records alone. It's certainly not a road that anyone wants to go down.

You may want to discuss your pending case with your supervisor or Human Resources department to find out how a reckless driving conviction might affect your job. You could also find out if a reduced outcome, such as a speeding conviction, would eliminate the employment risks.

Permanent criminal record

We discussed that reckless driving is a class 1 misdemeanor, but what does that really mean?

Virginia has three levels of offenses:

1. Traffic infractions - Charges such as speeding and running a stop sign fall in the traffic infraction group. They cannot be punished by jail time, and they are not crimes. They only go on your driving record.

2. Misdemeanors - These offenses are crimes. They go on your criminal record, and they can be punished by jail up to one year, depending upon the level of offense. Class 1 misdemeanors, like reckless driving, are at the top of the scale.

3. Felonies - These crimes carry possible jail time of more than one year. Fortunately, reckless driving is NOT a felony offense.

Now think about it: have you ever been asked about your criminal history on a job or security clearance application? You've probably been able to answer that you have no convictions. But if your reckless driving charge sticks, you must answer "yes" when asked if you've ever been convicted of a misdemeanor. Even life insurance applications sometimes ask about reckless driving convictions.

Just by receiving the reckless driving ticket, you've been charged with a misdemeanor. You will need to read applications carefully to see if they are asking about "charges" or "convictions." If they ask about misdemeanor charges, you have to answer "yes."

Unlike your driving record, the criminal record remains for life. Virginia doesn't even allow expungement (erasing the records later on) if the court convicts you.

Demerit points

Virginia has a complicated point system for drivers. Everyone starts out at zero. For every year of driving with no tickets, you get a +1 point. Positive points are good in Virginia. The best record has a +5 balance; that's the maximum number of allowable good points.

When Virginia DMV gets record of a moving violation conviction, they assess demerit points against you. Every moving violation carries a set number of points, either 3, 4, or 6.

Reckless driving carries the maximum number of demerit points for any offense in Virginia. If the court convicts you and you have a Virginia license, DMV will assess 6 demerit points. The conviction will remain on your driving record for 11 years.

If you accumulate too many demerit points too quickly, DMV may send you to a driver improvement clinic or suspend your license altogether.

If you have a license from another state, your home state controls the points you would get. For most states, Virginia will report any conviction to your home state. Then your state's DMV will determine if the conviction goes on your record, how long it stays there, and if you get demerit points for it.

3. What defenses are available?

Reckless driving charges can be beat. The Commonwealth has to prove beyond a reasonable doubt that you committed the alleged violation. Each piece of the offense can be used as a possible defense if the Commonwealth doesn't present the necessary evidence.

Since there are many possible defense angles in a reckless driving case, I can't cover every single one in a short book. Here are a few of the main defenses we might be able to mount against your charge.

Location

It sounds simple, but the Commonwealth has to prove that the offense took place in the correct county or city. In many cases, this is a formality, but not always.

Sometimes an incident may take place near the border between two localities, and it could be questionable exactly where the offense occurred.

Also, sometimes the officers make mistakes in their testimony. If they forget to testify that the incident occurred within the correct locality, we have a strong argument to have the judge dismiss the case completely.

Highway

The main reckless driving rules only apply on "highways." That is a complicated legal term that means much more than the interstate highway. However, not every roadway counts.

I had a client in Stafford County who was involved in a minor accident in a subdivision. Her responsibility for the accident was fairly cut and dried, and she received a reckless driving ticket. However, the road in question was part of a gated community, which made it a private road. Stafford County had not passed an ordinance to adopt the road as a legal "highway." Due to that issue, I was able to get the charge dismissed!

Driving

To support a reckless driving charge, the Commonwealth has to prove that YOU drove the vehicle. In many cases, they officer simply testifies that he stopped the vehicle and identified the driver by his/her driver's license.

However, the driving piece can occasionally be tricky for the Commonwealth to prove in accident cases, since the officer rarely observes the actual accident. Also, if someone stole your identity and incurred a ticket in your name, we'd certainly argue that you aren't the person who committed the offense.

In one case my client swore to me that he wasn't driving on the day in question. We checked the court paperwork, and the signature on the ticket didn't match his signature. The trooper confirmed that my client wasn't the driver he pulled over, and the case was dismissed.

Speed cases

Aside from the general elements of location, highway, and driving, reckless driving by speed charges have some specific potential defenses.

Speed limit

It may seem elementary, but the Commonwealth has the burden of proving the speed limit in question. Typically, that is straightforward, since Virginia law specifies the limits on many roads. However, that's not always the case.

One of my clients was charged with reckless driving in a school zone. The school zone signs were 35 mph. But I argued to the judge that 35 isn't the legal limit for a school zone, thus nullifying the signs. The judge ruled that the Commonwealth hadn't met its burden of proving the speed limit and dismissed my client's charge.

Radar / LIDAR calibrations

In any case where there's a question of speed, whether you're charged with speeding or reckless driving by speed, the Commonwealth has to prove that the device they used to measure your speed was calibrated and accurate on the day in question. And they have to prove it was calibrated within the past six months.

If the officer used a LIDAR gun, he should have a calibration certificate to show that the actual unit has been calibrated within six months prior to the stop. If he used a radar gun, he should have a calibration to show that his tuning forks were calibrated within that window.

The interesting thing about the statute and defending speed-related cases is that simply seeing a piece of paper that the officer claims is his certificate is not enough. The certificate has to meet the requirements in the statute to actually be able to prove that his device was accurate.

A traffic attorney should have the experience and knowledge to examine the officer's certificates and spot deficiencies. For example, the certificate must say who actually performed the calibration, and the certificate itself must be an original or a proper copy. Sometimes these deficiencies are so subtle that an inexperienced attorney could even miss them.

Your speedometer's calibration

Many "beat your ticket" books written by non-lawyers recommend calibrating your speedometer as a possible defense. I frankly don't recommend it in every case because it's not always helpful.

Having your speedometer calibrated attempts to show that even if the officer clocked you at X speed, you didn't realize you were going that fast. But that doesn't always work, since your speedometer might not be wrong. And not all judges will give you credit for a calibration.

Before you spend the money on an official calibration, you can do a quick accuracy test yourself with a GPS:

1. Put a standalone GPS in your car.
2. Set the GPS where it displays the current speed based on the GPS satellites.
3. Drive around a little and keep an eye on the GPS and speedometer readings.
4. If they consistently match, both gauges are probably showing the vehicle's true speed.

If you decide to get a calibration, you must know how to read a calibration report. I've seen many people say their calibration is helpful when it's actually the opposite. I've even seen defendants give the judge a calibration that shows their speedometer would've been reading higher than the officer alleges.

A typical calibration report is a notarized chart that shows the calibration machine's known speed compared with the speedometer's reading. The chart might look similar to this:

Machine	Speedometer
55 mph	52 mph
60 mph	57 mph
65 mph	62 mph

That example shows the vehicle's speedometer reading 3 mph lower than the actual travel speed of the car. That calibration would potentially be helpful in a reckless driving case.

In cases where your alleged speed falls on a borderline (like 80 mph) or if you truly believe your speedometer doesn't read correctly, a calibration may be useful for your defense.

The GPS defense

This one's my favorite!

I've seen people argue that their GPS showed a lower speed that the officer's radar, and I've had many clients tell me that as well.

Unfortunately, I think the GPS defense fails more often than it works. But that's because people don't bring all the necessary proof to court.

To effectively use a GPS defense in traffic court, you need two things: 1. proof of the GPS speed readout at the time the police claim you were speeding, and 2. proof that the GPS was accurate.

The GPS defense can be argued successfully, however. I argued this defense for a reckless driving client who had the presence of mind to take a picture of his GPS trip summary right after being pulled over for reckless driving. It showed the maximum speed during the trip was lower than the officer's radar reading. I had the client get his speedometer calibrated, and then I had him take pictures of the GPS and speedometer together to show that the GPS was reading accurately. The judge understood our argument and found that the defendant was only going the speed displayed as the GPS maximum speed.

General reckless driving

If your charge is under VA Code § 46.2-852 or § 46.2-853, it's probably because you were involved in an accident or the officer is just claiming that your driving was generally reckless. But the Commonwealth still has to prove that you drove in a way that endangered life, limb, or property.

Uncertainty provides our main defense in these kinds of cases. The officer can't just guess what happened. He needs evidence.

The Virginia Supreme Court has ruled that the mere happening of an accident isn't reckless driving. The Commonwealth has to be able to point to specific action or inaction by the driver that was reckless.

The main evidence against you in accident cases will probably be your own statements to the officer. People unknowingly incriminate themselves while telling the officer what happened. For example, simply saying that your tire slipped off the shoulder and you lost control can be enough for a judge to find you responsible for the accident.

But in a case where you didn't make any statements or your statements are vague, we may have a strong argument that the Commonwealth simply can't prove you were driving recklessly.

This is why attorneys always tell people not to talk. We mean it! If you don't say anything to the police, you won't provide statements that will be used against you at court.

Importantly, note that the accident report doesn't really matter in these cases. It's not admissible in court. It's basically a reporting tool for DMV's statistical purposes. Because of this, I counsel clients not to get hung up on errors or mistakes on the accident report. The officer's testimony in court is what really matters.

4. What defenses don't work?

By now you've probably read a lot about your reckless driving charge, and you may have heard defense ideas from friends and family as well. Here are a few mythical defenses that usually won't matter in court. Of course every case is different, but these don't work often in my experience.

If the officer doesn't show up, we win!

This might be the most common myth I hear. It comes up almost every day. In some states, this might be true. However, in Virginia, this isn't an automatic winner.

The officer normally has to be at court as the Commonwealth's witness for your case. But in most courts, the officer has one date per month where all his cases will be heard. That makes it easier for him to juggle his patrol duties and court schedule.

If the officer doesn't show up, most likely it will be due to a legitimate excuse. Everyone falls ill occasionally or has sudden family emergencies. And police officers have emergencies and unexpected calls due to their duties. In most courts, if an officer notifies the court with an excuse like any of these, his cases will simply be continued to his next court date. Not a win.

In a few rare instances, officers do forget or neglect court. If they don't show up and don't call the court, I certainly argue to the judge that the case should be dismissed. In those rare circumstances, the judge might agree. However, I have to emphasize that this doesn't happen often, and the judge still has the discretion to continue the case to another date.

The officer didn't stop everyone

I've heard many people argue this in court. Just the other day in Spotsylvania a guy was arguing that the car next to him was speeding too.

Unfortunately, it doesn't matter.

All that matters is if the officer can testify that he clocked your car (and all the other elements of the case, of course). He doesn't have to stop all speeders, and it would be impossible to even attempt that.

One of our local judges has responded to this argument by asking something like, "When you go fishing, do you catch all the fish in the lake?"

My car can't go that fast

This argument could matter, IF you could prove it.

The officer's testimony that his equipment read X speed presents the basic case against you. We can argue against that evidence with our own proof. If we could prove that your vehicle physically cannot go the alleged speed, that would be pretty convincing evidence that the officer's equipment must be wrong in your case.

However, how can we prove it? Your testimony wouldn't be enough for most judges. A printout from the internet wouldn't be admissible in court. We would really need an expert witness to testify about your particular vehicle. That could get pricey. In many cases, this argument simply won't help us.

It wasn't my car

In heavy traffic, it's reasonable to question if the officer clocked the correct vehicle. However, it's a hard argument to win.

In most cases, the officer is going to come into court and swear under oath that he clocked or paced a certain vehicle. He'll testify that he then stopped the car that he was targeting, and that he identified you as the driver with your driver's license. If he can say all that under oath, that's enough to establish the identity of the vehicle that's alleged to have committed the violation.

This is definitely an issue to examine closely, but it honestly doesn't normally help. The officer's testimony that he got the right car is usually sufficient for the judge.

My speedometer read 70

I'm in traffic court most mornings each week. It always surprises me how many people try this defense:

"But, Your Honor, I swear my speedometer only read 70!"

Most of the time the judge's next question is: "Did you get your speedometer calibrated or checked?"

And of course the defendant typically says "no."

The judge then convicts the defendant of speeding or reckless driving.

Why doesn't that work?

It all goes back to the basic elements for a reckless driving by speed case. If you're charged with reckless driving or speeding in Virginia, there are a few things the Commonwealth must prove to make a basic case against you:

1. The officer targeted your vehicle
2. The officer's radar / laser / speedometer read the alleged speed
3. The measuring device was properly calibrated

There are lots of other little elements they have to prove, but this is the basic case. Most judges defer to the officer's evidence when he's taken the oath and sworn that he clocked you.

You can certainly try to cast doubt upon the officer's basic case. That's the design of our criminal justice system. But to fight the exact speed the officer claims, you need more than your word that the speedometer read lower. A notarized calibration report for your speedometer can certainly be helpful to prove that, depending upon the judge. That's why many judges ask the defendant if they had their speedometer checked when this issue arises.

If you want to argue about what your speedometer read, a calibration is honestly a critical step.

I was going with the flow

I hear it all the time: "I was just going with the flow of traffic." I don't mean to be crass, but that's not going to matter. We have a lot of potential arguments and tactics to fight speeding and reckless driving charges, but this isn't one of them.

Virginia law prohibits exceeding the speed limit. There's no exception for "going with the flow."

What does that even mean? Was everyone going 100 miles per hour? Typically not. On Interstate 95 in the Fredericksburg / Spotsylvania / Stafford area, most people aren't even going 85 mph.

Maybe there are some other cars nearby who are traveling in the 80s. And maybe even a few cars driving in the 90s. But there are always cars driving closer to the speed limit.

This is a classic excuse of "everyone else was doing it." That doesn't work for children, and it doesn't work for speeding or reckless driving in Virginia.

The officer and the judge don't really care what other people were doing. They care if *you* were exceeding the speed limit.

I had to pee

When you've been in traffic court a lot, you've heard just about everything. You'd be amazed at how many people claim they were speeding because they had to pee.

Needless to say, this isn't a legal defense. It simply won't get you anywhere in the average case, especially if the officer testifies that you passed several exits with restrooms.

The only way this argument might help is if there's a special medical condition involved. Then some judges might consider it as mitigation for sentencing purposes.

5. What else can we do?

We've looked at the serious nature of reckless driving, some defenses that might be possible, and even which ones probably won't work. Your particular case may not seem hopeful at this point.

Fear not!

We still have options to resolve your case in a positive way.

First of all, you won't know all the possible defenses in your case without talking with an attorney. I'm not saying that everyone has to hire an attorney, but it only makes sense to have a free conversation to see what's possible in your case. Not all attorneys provide free consultations, but I do offer free consultations to people who have traffic charges in my local area. A traffic attorney who's local to your court can help you examine the facts of the case and give you a sense of what the judge might do.

Second, you don't have to be convicted of reckless driving even if you are technically guilty.

You read that right. Even in cases where the evidence is stacked up against us, we still have options!

Agreement with the officer

In case I haven't made it completely clear, officers have a lot of power in Virginia reckless driving cases.

But we can also try to use that power to our advantage. In some courts, the judge will consent to a recommendation or deal that the officer makes. Basically, that's because the officer is the person who was on scene and dealt directly with you. In theory, he has the best position to know what outcomes are reasonable in your case.

This doesn't mean officers will just roll over at court and drop your reckless driving charge. But it does mean that we might be able to work out a deal on your case to have it reduced to a lesser offense. Some factors that come into play are: your demeanor on the side of the road, the judge's willingness to accept recommendations from the officer, and your prior record. If you were uncooperative on the side of the road, the officer probably won't want to help you out at court. That's one reason I always recommend being polite to law enforcement officers.

Improper driving

Virginia law says that in any case of reckless driving where the culpability of the driver is minimal, the judge can reduce the charge to "improper driving."

What's "improper driving"? Improper driving is a 3-point traffic infraction. It disappears from your Virginia driving record in 3 years. It's one of the lowest-level moving violations in Virginia.

Improper driving can be a great result, compared to the 6-point misdemeanor conviction of reckless driving. Remember that reckless driving would be part of your permanent criminal record, but improper driving only goes on your driving record.

The judges around Fredericksburg, Stafford, and Spotsylvania use improper driving in many accident cases where the Commonwealth can prove responsibility for the accident, but where the defendant has minimal culpability. For example, if you were involved in a minor fender-bender, that might be a candidate for improper driving.

This is also an area where the officer has a lot of discretion. Virginia law doesn't allow officers to write improper driving tickets. They can only charge reckless driving. However, sometimes the officer will agree that improper driving fits the facts better. If the officer will agree to that, many judges will agree as well. At the very least, the officer can be questioned on cross examination if improper driving would be a more appropriate outcome.

No matter how we get there, improper driving beats reckless driving.

Driver improvement clinic

Even if the evidence is sufficient to find you guilty of reckless driving, the judge can still give you a break aside from improper driving. Virginia law allows the judge to send you to a driver improvement clinic to have a traffic case reduced or even dismissed completely. Note that this option is NOT available if you have a commercial driver's license.

Not all judges utilize this program, so it's important to find out what your judge likes to do. Some judges will dismiss certain speeds while reducing others. Some judges may not use driving school at all. Again, speak with a local attorney who knows the judge who will be handling your case to make sure you get solid advice.

Also, some judges don't like drivers doing a driving school before coming to court. That's because Virginia DMV awards five safe driving points for completing the driving school voluntarily. Some judges see that as double dipping. They don't want you to get five bonus points and then obtain a reduced charge in court. With those judges, doing driving school without consulting an attorney might hurt your case.

Community service

Along with improper driving and driving school, some judges use community service as a tool in traffic cases. It can be a way to punish defendants but also to give people a chance to earn a break on the charge.

Sometimes I recommend that clients complete some community service before their trial date. Doing volunteer work ahead of time shows initiative, remorse, and that you're taking the charge seriously. Depending upon the judge, this can help obtain a favorable result in court.

If the judge orders you to do community service for your case, be sure to pay close attention to the requirements. If in doubt, ask your attorney or the clerk's office. Around the Fredericksburg area, community service could be on your own at any non-profit charity, or it could be monitored through Community Based Probation. You certainly want to comply with the judge's specific orders.

6. What will happen at court?

Many people who receive a reckless driving ticket have never had to appear in court before. Even if you've been to court, you still may not know what to expect in the courtroom. It's daunting!

Here are some simple pointers about being in court for a reckless driving ticket.

Arraignment

Your first court appearance for a reckless driving case creates confusion for a lot of people. Is it an arraignment? Is it trial? What is arraignment anyway?

First off, what is arraignment? Arraignment is an initial hearing that is held in cases where jail time is a possible outcome. At arraignment, the judge explains that you're facing the possibility of jail, so you have the right to an attorney. The judge will explain three options:

1. You can hire your own attorney.
2. You can waive your right to an attorney.
3. You can ask for a court-appointed attorney. The court will only appoint an attorney if: A. you request one, and B. you qualify as "indigent," which means you have a low enough income (according to the state's formula) to show that you cannot afford to hire an attorney.

But will you have an arraignment?

Maybe, maybe not. Clear, right? That's unfortunately the way the legal system works.

Frankly, most reckless driving tickets aren't set for arraignment. Most likely, your case will be set directly for trial.

Around the Fredericksburg area, your case would normally be set for arraignment only at higher speeds, such as 100 mph in a 65 mph zone.

There are a few easy ways to determine if you're having an arraignment:

1. Check your ticket. It may say "arraignment" near the court date area. (See the sample in the Appendix.)
2. Call the court. The clerk's office can quickly tell you if you're set for arraignment or trial.
3. Call an attorney. I can usually tell people if they're set for arraignment simply based on the designated hearing time.

If you have an arraignment, once you tell the judge what you want to do about an attorney, he'll give you a trial date to come back to court. In some cases, if you waive your right to an attorney, the judge might ask if you want to simply have your trial that day; however, that isn't normally required.

After the arraignment, your next court date should be your actual trial date. What happens then?

Trial

If your case is not set for arraignment, it will be set immediately for trial (or an "adjudicatory" hearing). You'll get a full-fledged trial if you want it, but it's not like you've seen on television.

Do you have to appear?

Virginia tickets have a box underneath your signature that says "You may avoid coming to court only if this block is checked and all instructions on defendant's copy are followed." For most reckless driving cases, that box will NOT be checked, and many officers line through the text for good measure.

The default rule for reckless driving is that you have to appear in court. That's because it's a misdemeanor charge. You can't just prepay it and be done.

However, depending upon the specific case and the local court, an attorney may be able to appear on your behalf. I do this routinely for clients who are charged with reckless driving by speed at speeds less than 100 mph and 30 mph or less over the speed limit. For out of state drivers, this can save you time and travel expenses. Even for Virginia drivers, appearing in court can cost you an entire day's work; hiring an attorney can save your day off for something fun.

You should definitely consult with an attorney to determine if your appearance can be waived.

Who hears the case?

In Virginia, your first trial for a misdemeanor like reckless driving will take place in the General District Court (or Juvenile & Domestic Relations Court for juveniles).

Importantly, you don't get to have a jury trial in these courts (that's a possibility on appeal, which we'll cover in Chapter 7). All cases in General District Court are heard by a judge only. He'll decide if you're guilty beyond a reasonable doubt and what sentence to give you.

But it doesn't have to end there. If you're not happy with the outcome in your first trial, you have the absolute right to appeal the case for a brand new trial in the Circuit Court with a different judge (more on that in Chapter 7).

Will the prosecutor be involved?

Virginia calls the prosecutor the "Commonwealth's Attorney." They represent the Commonwealth in prosecuting crimes, like reckless driving. They are equivalent to the DA or "District Attorney" that some states have.

The Commonwealth's Attorney may or may not be involved in your case. It depends upon the nature of the reckless driving charge and the local court.

In many of Virginia's more rural jurisdictions, the prosecutor's office is too understaffed to handle every traffic offense that comes through the court. In those areas, they only get involved in the higher stakes offenses, such as reckless driving cases where they may want to seek jail time.

In cases where the prosecutor does not get involved, the ticketing officer will handle the case himself.

Knowing whether or not you'll be facing the Commonwealth's Attorney can be critical in your case. On one hand, they might know the law better than the officer. However, they also have wide discretion to negotiate plea agreements.

It always concerns me when I see non-local attorneys come into the Fredericksburg area courts, trying to find the prosecutor for cases where they don't get involved. Knowing who will be handling your case at court is a critical step in preparation and determining how to get the best possible result. This is yet another reason that I always recommend finding a local attorney who regularly handles cases like yours in the necessary court.

Act and dress appropriately

General District Courts are somewhat informal, especially compared to Virginia Circuit Court. However, it's still a court of law. The man in the black robe can send you to jail. Real jail.

When you're in court, whether or not you have an attorney, you should conduct yourself appropriately. That begins with dressing properly. I recommend at least business casual attire. For gentlemen, I recommend dress pants and a dress shirt. If ladies wear a skirt or dress, be sure to keep it conservative. Definitely do not wear shorts or revealing clothing.

Any time you're in the courthouse, be sure to be on your best behavior. The judges notice people who are rude and disruptive; you don't want to be noticed in that way.

Pay attention to the signs in the courthouse and follow all instructions by court personnel. For example, you probably won't be allowed to bring your cell phone or other electronics into the building. Also, some judges want you to answer verbally when your case is called; if you don't, your case may be passed until the end of the docket!

Be sure to ask courthouse personnel, or your attorney, to clarify any rules that are unclear so you are completely prepared for your court appearance.

Special accommodations

If you are handicapped, understand little or no English, or need other special accommodations in court, you should always contact the court in advance. Most Virginia courts have Spanish interpreters readily available, but other languages require advance planning. Other special accommodations may be able to be arranged in advance on a case-by-case basis.

The plea

When the judge calls your case, he'll most likely say something like this:

"Mr. Smith, you are charged with reckless driving, 89 in a 65 zone. How do you plead?"

You have three choices:

1. Guilty - admitting that you did it.
2. Not guilty - requiring the Commonwealth to prove it.
3. No contest - not fighting the evidence, but not admitting guilt.

If you look at the way I wrote those descriptions, there are subtle differences in each plea. Pleading guilty can end all discussion of the case, and the judge might proceed directly to sentencing. It's admitting that you are in fact guilty of reckless driving as charged. The judge may also ask if you have anything that you'd like to say about the case, which can give you a chance to ask for an alternate outcome.

Pleading not guilty doesn't mean you're innocent. It means that you are exercising your right to have a trial and confront the witnesses against you. Your trial will most likely begin right after you enter a "not guilty" plea (more on that in the next section).

A "no contest" plea fits in the middle, in my opinion. It admits that the Commonwealth can prove the charge, but it doesn't admit that you did in fact do what they claim. The judge may ask the officer for a brief overview of the facts, and you should have an opportunity to briefly say something about the charge.

The officer's testimony

If you plead not guilty, the judge will normally turn to the officer and ask him to talk about the case. The officer will then recite a fairly brief narrative of what happened. If the Commonwealth's Attorney is involved in the case, they may guide the officer through his testimony.

During the officer's testimony, you (or your attorney) can object to evidence he offers if there is a legal basis to do so. However, most of the time you should just listen carefully to what he says.

Once the officer finishes, it's your chance to ask him questions. You don't have to ask anything, but that's your one and only chance. If you do speak, be sure you're actually asking him a question. You'll get a chance to tell your side later.

Your testimony

You don't have to testify. You have the right under the Fifth Amendment to the U.S. Constitution to not incriminate yourself. But if you choose to say something about the case, you get a chance.

The judge will have you take the oath, and you'll get to talk. Be sure to keep it on target. I always tell my clients to keep it brief. The judge is busy, and he has many more cases to hear. Hit the high points and keep it to the facts.

Legal arguments

If you have hired an attorney, there may be a few other parts to your reckless driving trial. Sometimes there are pre-trial arguments to be made. For example, there may be an argument to keep out certain evidence or throw out the traffic stop altogether.

This is where your attorney's preparation truly shines. I work with my clients in advance to have the facts nailed down, and I research any applicable legal issues to be able to argue them on the spot in court.

One of my favorite arguments is what Virginia calls a "motion to strike." After the Commonwealth's evidence is submitted (typically just the ticketing officer's testimony), the Commonwealth must have laid out a basic case that you committed reckless driving. They need to have all the pieces on the table. If they're missing a piece at that point, we can argue that the judge should dismiss the case right then. And if a critical piece (such as radar calibrations) was omitted, we should win!

At the end of the case, there will usually be a final argument. This is where you argue something like reasonable doubt.

While you can argue a motion to strike or closing argument yourself, these are definitely areas where having an attorney can pay off. A local traffic attorney should know how the judge responds to certain types of arguments and how to best craft those arguments for your unique case.

Sentencing

If the judge finds the evidence is enough to support some conviction (either reckless driving or a lesser offense, like improper driving), he'll need to impose a sentence.

There may be a brief argument at this point about attending driver improvement, doing community service, or maybe some other alternative punishment. However, this is where the rubber meets the road. Once the sentence is handed down, the case is over.

Fine, jail, and getting home

If you owe any money in fines and costs to the court, you have at least 30 calendar days to pay. The clerks may require you to sign a form before you leave, but you don't have to pay anything on your court date. If you don't pay on time, your license will be suspended for non-payment.

If you get jail time, you will be immediately put in the custody of the sheriff to serve your time. Fortunately, we have options to delay that when necessary. A local attorney will be familiar with the local court system and can help you setup your jail time to fit around your work schedule.

If the judge suspends your license, it normally gets suspended immediately upon conviction. If you don't have someone to drive you home, some judges will delay the suspension so you can get home. You should be sure to speak with your attorney and/or the clerk's office to understand when your suspension goes into effect and if you have permission to drive home.

That's it. Or is it?

7. Appealing the case

As we talked about, your first trial for a Virginia reckless driving ticket happens in the General District Court (assuming you're an adult).

If you are unhappy with the outcome of your case, you have the absolute right to appeal it to the Circuit Court. This is called a "de novo" appeal, which means everything starts all over. You get a brand new trial with a different judge.

It's a powerful right!

Filing your appeal

The most important thing to remember about appealing your case: you MUST file the appeal within 10 calendar days after trial. Note: this deadline is not based on business days. The appeal deadline is based on calendar days, so weekends are included!

If you wait more than 10 calendar days, you're out of luck. No more appeal. It's a powerful tool, but you have to act fast.

Actually filing the appeal requires a single piece of paper in most courts. Simply tell the General District Court clerk that you want to appeal, and they'll give you a Notice of Appeal form (a sample is in the Appendix). They'll usually fill out the main data for you and have you sign it. That's it.

The Notice of Appeal form will say that you have to appear in Circuit Court on a certain date to either have your new trial or pick a trial date. Whichever it says, be there! If you don't appear as scheduled, you will probably be charged with failure to appear, another misdemeanor. Even if you don't get jail time for your reckless driving charge, you could go to jail for failing to appear in Circuit Court.

Your appeal trial

The appeal trial happens the same way as the original trial did. The officer testifies, you can ask questions, you can testify, etc.

You also have the right to an attorney, even if you're not facing jail time. If you didn't hire an attorney the first time around, it might make sense to hire someone for the appeal to try to get a better result.

The appeal trial has two main differences from the original trial:

1. You have the right to a jury trial. But be careful when demanding a jury, since if you're

convicted you'll have to pay for it. In some courts, that costs around $1,000.

2. The Commonwealth's Attorney will almost certainly be involved. Even in the areas I handle where the prosecutor doesn't handle reckless driving cases, they do get involved on appeals. The prosecutor normally gets involved at this level mainly because there are fewer appeals, so they have the manpower to handle it. As we talked about before, this can be good or bad, depending upon your case. Sometimes if a case doesn't go well in General District Court, the Commonwealth's Attorney will negotiate a reduced plea agreement in Circuit Court.

Withdrawing your appeal

What happens if you appeal your case and then change your mind?

No problem. You can withdraw the appeal!

Virginia lets you withdraw the appeal any time before your new trial begins. If you decide to withdraw before your Circuit Court appearance date, you can easily do that at the clerk's office. If you wait until you appear in Circuit Court, you can tell the judge that you want to withdraw when he asks for a plea.

When you withdraw an appeal, the General District Court result becomes effective. That means the outcome will be put on your driving record, and you have to do whatever the punishment was. If the judge imposed jail time, you would be taken into custody right when you withdraw the appeal.

The only thing that can change with the withdrawn appeal is that you might pay more in court costs. If you withdraw within the first 10 days after trial, you only pay the original court costs. However, if you wait more than 10 days, the Circuit Court gets the case file. Once they have the file, you have to pay their court costs as well. This can add about another $100 to your total bill.

8. How to pick an attorney

By now you hopefully have a solid grasp of reckless driving law, potential defenses, practical aspects of appearing in court, and what alternative outcomes may be possible. Thanks for reading this far!

You may not need an attorney for your reckless driving charge. But I always recommend talking to the right attorney to find out what you're facing, what can be done for your case, and if hiring counsel makes sense.

Note that I said you should talk to the RIGHT attorney. How do you know who that might be? You want an attorney who is properly equipped to get a great result in your unique case. Let's look at several questions you should ask ANY attorney when you interview them for your reckless driving case.

Who will be defending me in the courtroom?

When you buy a car, you look for the precise vehicle that best fits your needs. When you take delivery, you ensure that it's exactly the vehicle you paid for.

Hiring an attorney should be the same way. You spend considerable time reading up on the law, checking into attorneys, talking to them, and then you hire someone.

But when crunch time comes, who will be standing there with you in court? That's the precise moment you're concerned about.

You may be surprised to learn that lots of firms pass files to more junior associates or "of counsel" attorneys. You might read one attorney's writing on the website, talk to another attorney on the phone, and be standing next to an attorney you've never heard of when you get to court.

When you hire me, you get me. I'm the only attorney in my office, and I'll be the person defending you in court. Clients hire me because they want my experience and knowledge put to use in their case. I wouldn't think of passing a client off to anyone else.

If someone calls for a county that I don't handle or a case that cannot fit into my calendar, I decline the case. Instead of taking your money and shuffling you off to someone else, I do my best to connect you with a trusted colleague who you can hire to defend the ticket.

Do you EVER pass your clients off to other attorneys?

This question relates to the previous one, but it's an even more serious concern, in my opinion.

Some attorneys spread themselves thin and take on cases that conflict with already-scheduled court dates. Instead of carefully managing their calendar to ensure they can personally handle every case, some attorneys ask colleagues to "stand in" for a case in court.

I know. I've been asked by several of my competitors to stand in for them. Usually, the "stand in" attorney gets contacted a few days before trial and asked to add a case to their calendar. The attorney YOU paid to defend your case might fax a copy of the file to the "stand in" guy, or he might not. Then a random attorney who isn't even associated with your attorney appears in court for your case.

Again, if you hire me, I handle your case in court. I've NEVER had someone else appear in court for a client, and I don't plan to ever do that.

Where are you located?

Reckless driving defense varies a LOT based on the local court, judges, prosecutors, officers, etc. I always recommend looking for a local attorney who regularly handles reckless driving cases in the court where your charge is pending.

Be sure to ask the attorney where his PRIMARY office is located. Quite a few lawyers have "satellite offices" located around the Commonwealth. This can make it look like they're local to the court you need, when in reality, they are from another area altogether.

My office is located in Spotsylvania County, off Exit 126 on Interstate 95. I live in Spotsylvania County as well.

Spotsylvania County is right next door to the City of Fredericksburg and Stafford County. The Fredericksburg / Stafford / Spotsylvania area is essentially a mini-metropolitan area.

Here are the distances from my office to the nearby courts:

Spotsylvania General District	*5.7 miles*
Fredericksburg General District	*5.6 miles*
Stafford General District	*13.9 miles*

I also defend cases in King George, Caroline, and Orange, but I am primarily in the above courts.

What percentage of your practice is devoted to traffic and misdemeanor defense?

If you're getting brain surgery done, you want a brain surgeon. If you're getting advice from an attorney, you want to be talking to somebody who handles a lot of reckless driving charges.

One trend among law firms these days relies on having separate websites for each area of law they handle. You might come across a website that talks solely about reckless driving defense and think that the attorney handles nothing else. That's their goal. But if you Google the attorney's name, you might find that they have, for example, a family law website or a personal injury website as well.

It's difficult to dabble in any area of the law, since there can be many traps for the unwary. Finding an attorney who focuses on exactly your need helps to ensure he has the experience and tools to get the best result possible. Remember the old saying, "Jack of all trades, master of none."

My ENTIRE practice is devoted to traffic and misdemeanor defense. I do nothing else. Period.

You won't find me handling family law cases or doing bankruptcies. I don't do civil appeals or personal injury claims. I'm routinely asked to handle lots of different matters, and I decline that business.

I have focused my practice like a laser beam so I can hone my craft and serve my traffic and misdemeanor defense clients to the best of my abilities.

How often do you handle reckless driving cases in this court?

Just being located near the court you need isn't sufficient. Neither is focusing on traffic defense. I recommend talking to an attorney who regularly handles reckless driving cases in the court where your case is pending.

It's all about specific experience in the right courtroom. I've mentioned several times that these cases differ greatly based on the court. Even if someone handles ten reckless driving cases every week in Richmond or Fairfax, they may not have the first clue about what the judge will do in your case in Spotsylvania. The judges, officers, prosecutors, and local procedures all vary between courts. You should seek out someone who knows the court where your case will be heard.

I regularly defend reckless driving charges in Spotsylvania, Stafford, and Fredericksburg. I defend drivers in the local courts four or five days a week.

I get calls from potential clients for cases all over Virginia, but I don't take on those clients. You deserve an attorney who knows the local court, and I focus on the areas that I know.

Will the Commonwealth's Attorney be involved in my case?

As I discussed earlier, there may or may not be a prosecutor in your case. That can affect the preparation of the case before court and the strategy in the courtroom. You want an attorney who knows what players will be involved in your case and can properly prepare for trial.

When we talk about the facts of your case, we can discuss if the prosecutor will be involved or not. For the most part on reckless by speed cases, they do not get involved in Fredericksburg area cases where the speed is less than 100 mph and the speed is less than 30 mph over the limit. However, that does vary on a case-by-case basis.

Do you know the ticketing officer?

Having a working relationship with the ticketing officer can be critical in reckless driving defense. The officer's discretion can hurt or help your case. When at all possible, it makes sense to hire an attorney who is familiar with the officers in the court where your case is pending.

I have worked hard to develop professional, working relationships with the traffic officers, deputies, and troopers in my local area. I can't say that I know everyone, but I hope that everyone knows my reputation as a man of integrity, an attorney who gets results, and a nice guy.

Which judge will be hearing my case?

This is one of those details like the Commonwealth's Attorney's involvement: it can be important for preparing the case, and it shows if the attorney is familiar with the court. Of course, knowing the name of the judge isn't enough to know what might happen with your case. However, NOT knowing the possible judges can show a lack of familiarity.

No one can guarantee what judge will be on the bench for your reckless driving charge. However, I know all of the regular local General District Court judges. When we talk about your case, I'll tell you which judge would normally be hearing your trial.

When I get to court to handle cases, I confirm which judge is actually on the bench. If it's an unexpected judge or a substitute, I re-examine my case strategy to see what might need to change to get the best result possible.

Are you familiar with the judge's habits with driving school and alternative outcomes?

Once you know which judge is likely to hear your case, you should question what that judge does with cases like yours. Every case is unique and depends upon the specific facts, but attorneys can have a general feel for the judge based on past experience.

Most judges have informal policies about how they handle reckless driving charges. For example, they may accept driving school at certain speeds to dismiss the case completely. They might accept it in other types of cases to earn a reduction to a regular speeding ticket. As an example, one local judge doesn't send anyone over 25-years-old to driving school.

These differences can dramatically impact the approach to your case. Thus, it's critical for your attorney to know the judge's normal policies.

One of the main issues we'll talk about during a free consultation is what the judge might do with the facts of your case. That doesn't guarantee what will happen in court, but we will definitely talk about the judge's leanings so you can get an idea of what to expect.

Do you know the clerks?

Some attorneys practically ignore the clerks at the courthouse. I think that's wrong. They're people too. And they also have the power to make your case a little smoother.

For example, if your license gets suspended, you may need to apply for a restricted license. Preparing the license can take the clerks a few business days, which means you wouldn't be able to drive at all for a while. But sometimes the clerks can speed that process up to get you back on the road more quickly.

I've tried to get to know all the local traffic / criminal General District Court clerks. Simply learning people's names and greeting them when I appear in court goes a long way. Developing a professional relationship with people like the clerks helps to ensure a smooth court experience.

Do you have testimonials from previous clients that I can read?

If you're looking to hire any professional, you should ask for references or examples of past work. It's a little bit tricky for attorneys to provide information like that due to client confidentiality. However, Virginia attorneys are definitely allowed to provide testimonials and reviews from prior clients (subject to certain rules by the state regulators).

Testimonials certainly shouldn't be used as the sole way to evaluate an attorney. But if an attorney doesn't have any testimonials from satisfied clients, that may be a red flag. I'd also be concerned if an attorney was simply reluctant to answer this question or tried to side-step it.

I'm blessed to have dozens of testimonials and reviews from past clients. I've included a handful here in this book. You can view and listen to others on my website and on websites such as Google Maps and Yelp. These testimonials are not edited for grammar or spelling.

> "Working with Andrew Flusche has been great. I live far from where I needed to attend court, and he did a great job keeping in touch with me. My final charges were very less severe theni had thought, he helped greatly."
> --Michelle

> "I was amazed at how smoothly my problem was handled. We were able to conduct our business by phone and computer. I did not even have to go to court. Andrew handled everything for me. What a relief!"
> Carol

> "Andrew provided excellent service, answering all my questions and handling the situation in a professional manner. His contact with me was superb, including a telephone call immediately after court decision was rendered."
> --Ken

"Andrew Flusche handled my case in a thoroughly professional and cost efficient manner. He resolved the matter favorably and the outcome was as he predicted."
--Thad

You can read more testimonials on my website: www.AndrewFlusche.com/Testimonials/

There are certainly other factors to consider when talking with attorneys for your case, but these give you a good overview of what to look for. More subtle areas such as personality and how well you connect with each other can also be incredibly important in selecting the right attorney for your case.

9. Resources

This section holds a few tidbits of information that may be useful in navigating your reckless driving case.

Calibration shops

If you need to get your speedometer calibrated, it's important to take it to a shop that can do it right and provide the proper notarized calibration sheet. These shops can do that.

Falls Run Car Care
1314 Princess Anne St
Fredericksburg, VA
(540) 899-6800

Burton's Automotive
1443 Warrenton Rd
Fredericksburg, VA
(540) 752-5761

M&M Collision
3165 Campbell Drive
Fairfax, VA
(703) 591-9601

Southern Electronics
730-A Research Rd
Richmond, VA
(800) 446-2880

Court contact information

If you've lost the details for the court you have to appear in, don't panic. You can find all the details for any General District Court in Virginia right on the Supreme Court's website:

courts.state.va.us/courts/gd.html

Driving schools

Earlier I mentioned possibly doing a driving school or improvement class before your case. Here are some schools you could use. But definitely talk with a good attorney first, because doing a course before your court date could HARM your case in some instances.

Virginia's list of approved driver improvement clinics:
www.dmvnow.com/webdoc/citizen/drivers/clinics.asp

I usually recommend this online clinic:
www.iDriveSafely.com/Virginia

10. What's next?

Thank you for reading my book. Now you should have a good overview of your reckless driving case and how to hire an attorney.

Even if you don't think you want to hire an attorney, I suggest you call a good attorney. Most lawyers, including myself, offer free initial consultations. It doesn't cost you anything to talk to a solid traffic defense attorney to get some advice on your unique case.

If you'd like to talk to me about a case in my area, give me a call any time: 540.318.5824.

Good luck!

"Everything involved with my case was handled in a professional and timely matter, I couldn't be happier with the entire process and its outcome."
--Dominic

About Andrew

I focus on defending traffic cases in the Fredericksburg, Spotsylvania, Stafford area in Virginia. I run my own law firm with the help of my wonderful wife and my excellent legal assistant.

I was born and raised in North Texas, living in the same house from birth until I went to college at the University of Dallas. I met my wife at college, and we got married after graduation. Then we made the trek to Virginia for me to attend law school at the University of Virginia.

Throughout college and law school, I paid the bills as an internet programmer. I still enjoy programming, and I use those skills to build programs to efficiently manage my firm.

After graduating from UVA, my wife and I moved to Spotsylvania County, where I began my practice. I focus on providing top notch client service while relieving stress and obtaining the best possible resolution in court.

When I'm not at court, I enjoy spending time with my wife and road bicycling.

Appendix

Virginia Uniform Summons

This is an example of Virginia's ticket format. If you receive one, it would likely be a yellow carbon copy.

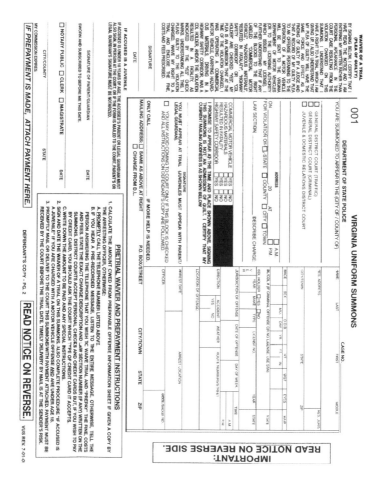

Notice of Appeal

If you appeal your General District Court trial, the clerk's office should prepare a form similar to this one. This form is a sample only.

NOTICE OF APPEAL — CRIMINAL.
Commonwealth of Virginia VA. CODE §§ 16-1-132, 16-1-133

Case Number(s)

.... General District Court

CITY OR COUNTY

NOTICE OF APPEAL.

DATE OF CONVICTION OR BAIL DETERMINATION

I, the undersigned, appeal [ ] my conviction [ ] the determination on bail to the Circuit Court of this city or county. I understand that this appeal may be withdrawn at any time prior t the hearing date set form my case. My appeal is scheduled to be called for [ ] hearing on appeal of determination of bail [ ] trial [ ] setting of trial date on

APPELLANT'S NAME (LAST, FIRST, MIDDLE)

.... in the Circuit Court, which is located at

ADDRESS

STREET ADDRESS OF CIRCUIT COURT

WORK .... TELEPHONE NUMBER .... HOME

TELEPHONE

I understand that if this is an appeal of a conviction and it is withdrawn within 10 days after my conviction in this District Court, no additional costs will be taxed against me; otherwise, additional costs will be incurred in Circuit Court. I also understand that upon withdrawal of that appeal, I am subject to the terms of my sentence.

WITHDRAWAL.

I, the undersigned, withdraw my appeal in this case

WARNING— You are subject to trial and conviction in your absence if you fail to appear for your trial in the Circuit Court. Failure to appear for your trial shall be deemed a waiver of your right to trial by jury in this case. Failure to appear may also constitute a separate criminal offense.

by ....
ATTORNEY FOR APPELLANT

I promise to appear before the Circuit Court of this jurisdiction at the date and time shown.

by ....
DATE OF APPEAL

APPELLANT

COURT USE ONLY

[ ] Release on $ ....

by ....
ATTORNEY FOR APPELLANT

$ ....

[ ] Not eligible for bail.

NOTICE: Promptly communicate with the Clerk of the Circuit Court of this jurisdiction concerning the subpoenaing of witnesses and any need for interpreters, concerning your right of representation by a lawyer if you do not have a lawyer, and, if you are appearing a conviction, if you wish to request a jury trial. If your case is scheduled for trial, you MUST be present and ready for trial at the "date and time of appearance" shown above.

FORM DC-370 REVISED 7-05

Index